7 SECRETS OF THE RICH

Lawrence G. Samuel

Understanding Money

7 SECRETS OF THE RICH

"Don't Spend Money Send Money"

Written by

Lawrence G. Samuel

Your freedom from financial lockdown

What People are saying about This Book.

The book has great depth. It's not the conventional book you read on finance, which makes it stand in a class of its own. It's highly recommended for all that are intentional about their financial journey.

~Lesi Nwasigbo CEO, WriteUp Africa

While entrepreneurship may not be for everyone, investments should be a priority and lifestyle for all and sundry, whether as employees or business owners. Why is this so? This is because investment is one secure way to financial freedom and stability. This book avails you some life nuggets to living a debt free life and creating a trans-generational wealth. The author has expounded thoughtfully and practically steps to guide us all. I will encourage young people, especially young adults to make the most use of every thought shared herein either as graduates, job seekers, working professionals and millenials (gen X & Y); putting in the work, noting that time will surely reward our efforts. Cheers to life and business success.

~Daniel Kolapo Emmanuel (Human Capital Strategist)

I found "7 Secrets of the Rich" to be a treasure box of financial wisdom necessary for birthing my financial freedom. It has helped to broaden and remold my understanding of money contrary to the conventional financial legacy I inherited from my predecessors. And I have come to discover that entrepreneurship guided by financial intelligence is the highest leveraged career path if I am going to join the train of the rich.

~Delight Oyelola (Abuja, Nigeria)

This Book is on a whole new level, its concept about what money is, is so captivating.

~Bodunde Steve S. (Hefei, Anhui Province, China)

I have deeply read this book "7 Secrets of the Rich", and I am deeply impacted by its simplicity, honesty and clarity on how just everyone can understand how money works! The author schooled me afresh on how the rich stay rich and the poor stay poor and went ahead to methodically chart the course to becoming rich no matter the current financial status. It is an awesome book for those who want to be financially literate and free.

~David Odiba (Transformational speaker and Author; The Leading Leader)

SuccessPlanet Inc.

DEDICATION

I dedicate this book to my loving father of blessed memory and to the millions of people out there struggling financially. May this book become the source of your financial turn-around.

ACKNOWLEDGEMENT

My deepest gratitude goes to the Almighty God the source of all inspiration.

Special thanks to my friend and editor Lesi Nwasigbo, who motivated me to put my thoughts in print. Your contributions and willingness to help made this project possible.

To my dear friends Edeh Anayo, Amarachi Ihejirika, Delight Oyelola, and Pastor David Odiba, thanks for your encouragement and constant checking up on the progress of this project.

To every member of my review and launching team, you guys did a great job.

To Mummy Dosunmu, Mrs. Christiana Lawrence, Daddy Agboola, and Mrs. Patience Madu, I say a big thank you for your parental guidance. And to my siblings, Sister Modupe and Sister Funmi, Michael and Glory, I love you all.

Finally, many thanks to all the members of RCCG; Hope of Glory Parish, for affording me the time to put this together.

CONTENTS

INTRODUCTION

No Money

A lot of us never cared about money until we got to High School. This is because kiddies' years are characterized by innocence, reliance on parents, ignorance and irresponsibility. The empathy and rapid response displayed by our parents whenever we sound our ecstatic need ringtone: 'mummy, daddy, please buy this for me', is so satisfying, as they usually feel obliged to always meet our every need.

We thought it was ever going to be so until we got to High School and the rules changed. The all-need-satisfying mum and dad suddenly became "no money" parents. You say something like,

"Mum, I need money for textbooks"

Mum says "no money".

"Dad, I need money for my school fees",

Dad says "no money" or "wait till month end".

And you say, "Ok, how about my lunch money?"

And they both say, "Eat well before you leave home son."

That sounds funny, right?! I know you can relate.

With their repressing responses, no sooner the reality of "no money" problem dawns on you contrary to your childhood fantasy experience.

Growing up, I used to think the "no money" problem is just about my parents until I met some friends in High School who rarely ever had money to pay for stuff. I remember my first day in High School, during break-time; I brought out my lunch box to eat, after about two scoops, a classmate who barely ever knew me for 5 hours, collected my meal and ate. Yeah! You read that right. Whether out of "no money" or whatever, all I knew is that she ate my first-day-at-school meal. Again, Tunde and I went to the grocery store; I bought some snacks and asked my friend,

"Aren't you buying?

He replied, "No money".

I said, "Oh, that's fine. We share then".

Just when I thought my parents were the only "no-money" parents, I didn't know "no-money" folks exist everywhere; in school, church, on our streets, in the neighbourhood, offices and even in the hospitals.

My study about money began, as I observed people everywhere say "no money" including my father who had once worked with the Nigeria's Printing and Minting Company.

Baffled by this general problem, one day, while in class, I asked my Economics Teacher, Mrs. Salvador,

I said "ma, why do people complain of no-money while an institution created to print money exists. Can't the firm be directed to print more money so that everyone would have just enough to spend?"

She gave me a smile that suggests, *welcome to the world of no-money, boy!*

"If nations are to print money just because her people lack it, life will not be balanced", she said to me.

That reply sounds ambiguous. What does she mean by life will not be balanced, I said to myself. Upon further study, light came upon me and my ignorance vanished. I realized money is not just a piece of paper that can be printed on privation or scarcity but a representation (unit) of value. Thus, printing more money without attaching a value to it would only reduce the worth of the currency (more money less production) leading to inflation. And an inflated economy is an unstable economy. This is what I found out.

Hmm, if printing more money will not solve the no-money problem, what then would – my quest lingered.

While I keep searching for answers I stumbled upon an old adage common amongst my people "ise l'ogun ise. Which been translated as work is the antidote for poverty. In context, it means, 'hard' work is the solution to no-money problem. While this may be true to some extent, the money is only temporal not permanent and most times petty. May it interest you to know that, according to survey, the most hard-working people on earth are the poor.

If this be the case, why then are the poor still poor?

What is the secret code to unlock wealth?

As you journey through this book, you will find out.

This book explains money in its most relatable sense. It outlines seven (7) powerful secrets capable of making just anyone rich, and it classifies money with regards to man into three categories; The Rich, The Poor and Middle-Class each with its own distinctive characteristics. You want to know what makes the poor poor, and the secret code to riches? You just found the right key.

PART ONE

MAKING MONEY

CHAPTER ONE

What is Money?

"Human history is, in essence, a history of ideas."

H.G. Wells

When you hear 'money', what first comes to your mind? Coins, paper, or some digital currency – if that is all you know about money probably, that explains why money is far from you or not with you, because you know little or nothing about it. To have money, you need to make money your friend; you need to know about money. The success of any friendship is established upon knowledge. What you know or don't know about money goes a long way to determining whether you will eventually have it.

There is more to money than you already know. This chapter is divided into two sections, each with valuable information and insights to broaden your horizon and help you understand the difference between what could be money and what money truly is.

So, let's begin!

Section One

What could be money?

Money could be a shell, a precious stone, a metal coin, or a piece of paper with a historic image on it, or any object that is generally accepted in the trade market for exchanging goods and services. Money, in and of itself, is nothing. It has no value unless the value is attributed to it by the traders, government, or financial institutions.

This means that money derives its value by being a medium of exchange and a unit of measurement. It is a medium of exchange, because you can get what you want through purchase and a unit of measurement because it measures the worth of an intrinsic value with its corresponding face value so nobody feels cheated.

The importance of money as a measure of value cannot be over-emphasized. You know how it hurts when you pay more for less or you're paid less for more. Somewhat, the evolution of money has really helped to minimize that loss. With money, virtually everything has a price. So, it became easy to trade items, skills, goods, properties, services, knowledge, information, etc. in exchange for money. Empirically, there is nothing you want to get or do today that involves others that does not require money. So the saying goes, money answers all things.

Again, money can be anything that is commonly accepted by a group of people as a medium of exchange. Note the word *exchange* – the law of exchange is not valid with an individual at least two people must be involved for an exchange to exist. So, having money does not automatically mean you own or have a shoe, dress, car, food or personal computer; you have to exchange it with someone in possession of those values before they become yours. Thus, having all the fait money in this world and not exchanging it for a value is useless.

In business and economics the word exchange can be interchanged with trade. Trading means exchanging a value for another value; it is like, you give me a piece of land and I give you gold, or you give me bread, I give you money – exchanging value with value.

If money is therefore a value that can be exchanged for another value, it thus implies that money can be just anything of value that can be traded. Not only commodities like, food items, cars, houses, accessories can be exchanged for money. Your gifts, talent, look, voice, skills, knowledge; anything at all of value or that gives value is passive money in a particular sense. Hence, when you see a man that lacks money check whether there is exchange of value going from him to another – without exchange of value you're literally on your own; poor.

Money is the line that differentiates the rich from the poor, the great from the small, and the strong from the weak. Money is your passport to the world. Without it you are in your own world.

How did we get to this point?

To fully understand the concept of money let's take a deep dive into its history, where it came from, and what purpose it was created to serve.

History of Money
The ancient origins of economic systems and invention of money predates the beginning of written history. It is impossible to trace the true origin of the invention of money because history has been severed by wars, migrations, natural disasters, and with ancient civilizations developing at different paces, proper records were not kept.

Consequently, any book or story that tries to explain how money first developed is largely based on conjecture and logical inference.

However, while needs and wants exist, man developed a system of exchange called "Trade by Barter." This is the earliest means of transaction according to history.

Trade by Barter

Bartering is a direct trade of goods and services. The Barter System involves giving out what you have to get what you want. I'll give you yam if you can give me a fish or I will build you a hut if you give me a sheep.

With barter, an individual possessing any surplus of value, such as a measure of grain or a quantity of livestock, could directly exchange it for something perceived to have similar or greater value or utility, such as a chair or a tool. However, the capacity to carry out barter transactions is limited in that it depends on a coincidence of wants.

For example, a farmer has to find someone who would not only want the grain he produced but who could also offer something in return that the farmer wants. This system of trade still exists today. People trade expensive jewelries for mobile phones. Landed properties can be exchanged for a car or house. A cow can be traded for food items and so on. The bartering system has really been helpful especially in areas of perishable commodities.

Commodity Money

Due to the limitation of transaction in the bartering system, an advanced system was developed called commodity money. Commodity money is the use of items that have value in themselves like cowries, salt, cattle, metal to trade. Many cultures around the world developed the use of commodity money. The ancient China, Africa, and India used cowry shells. In Western Asia (formerly called Mesopotamia) the shekel was used as the unit of weight and currency.

Metals, where available, were preferred as proto-money over such perishable commodities as cattle, cowry shells, or salt, because these metals were precious, durable, portable, and easily divisible. Internationally, metals, because of its characteristics, became widely the acceptable money.

The evolution of metals marked the birth of the monetary system. Even in the Bible, the first use of money was recorded in the Book of Genesis and it referenced silver as the medium of exchange.

Monetary System

Coins and Currency

The development of coin money began as men started to trade items for metals due to its endearing nature. The use of gold as proto-money has been traced back to the Fourth Millennium BC when the Egyptians used gold bars of a set weight as a medium of exchange as had been done earlier in Mesopotamia with silver bars. Sometime around 770 B.C., the Chinese moved from using random metallic tools and weapons as a medium of exchange to using miniature replicas of the same tools cast in bronze.

As some of these metallic objects are not hand friendly, the need to reshape and resize them into less harmful and tangible substance arose. So, circular coins were invented. Although China was the first country to use recognizable coins, the first minted coins were created not too far away in Lydia (now Western Turkey).

In 600 B.C., Lydia's King Alyattes minted the first official currency. The coins were made from electrum, a mixture of silver and gold that occurs naturally, and stamped with pictures that acted as denominations. By this time, coin money has evolved from just being a unit of weight to being a unit of value. Lydia's currency helped the country increase both its internal and external trade, making it one of the richest empires in Asia Minor. It is interesting that when someone says, "as rich as Croesus", they are referring to the last Lydian king who minted the first gold coin.

The spread of coin money was also aided by a process called *assaying*. Assaying is the analysis for the determination of the chemical composition of metals. Any soft metal, such as gold, can be tested for purity on a touchstone. Where alloys of gold are been used as money, a touchstone allows the amount of gold in the coin to be estimated. In turn, the intrinsic value of the coin is determined and a face value allocated to it.

Coins were typically minted by governments and then stamped with an emblem that guaranteed the weight and value of the metal. Sometimes, they reduce the amount of precious metal in the coin (reducing the intrinsic value) and yet assert the same face value just like the coin money we have in our present day world.

Banknotes
In the seventh century, just when it looked like Lydia was taking the lead in currency developments, the Chinese moved from coins to paper money. Paper money was introduced in Song Dynasty China during the 11th Century. The development of the banknote began as people's needs became more refined, indirect exchange became more likely, as the physical separation of skilled labourers (suppliers) from their prospective clients (demand) required the use of a medium common to all communities, to facilitate a wider market.

Also, merchants and wholesalers desired to avoid the carriage of heavy bulk of coin money across borders in large commercial transactions and international trades for safety reasons. Local safes (similar to modern day banks) were created which allowed business men to store their coins and a receipt or credit note was issued to them as proof of deposit. This credit note, otherwise known as banknote nevertheless, did not replace coins during the Song Dynasty; paper money was used alongside the coins.

The central government soon observed the economic advantages of printing paper money, issuing a monopoly right of several of the deposit shops to the issuance of these certificates of deposit. By the early 12th Century, the amount of banknotes issued in a single year amounted to an annual rate of 26 million strings of cash coins.

Until the 16th Century, the Europeans were still using coin money. The first European banknotes were issued by Stockholms Banco, a predecessor of Sweden's Central Bank Sveriges Riksbank. In 1661, banks started using banknotes for depositors and borrowers to carry around instead of copper-plate coins being used as a means of payment.

These notes could be taken to the bank at any time and exchanged for their face values in silver or gold coins. This paper money could be used to buy goods and pay for services, but it was issued by banks and private institutions, not the government. Just like the modern day ATM cards issued by banks that allow you access to your stored money, the banknotes have a similar function.

In the 19th Century in the United States, more than 5,000 different types of banknotes were issued by various commercial banks in America. To curb the proliferation of too many banknotes in the market issued by various financial institutions, government of different nations resolved on having a singular representative note called *currency*. Hence, the issuance was lifted from banks and committed to the government.

Today, virtually all countries have their national currency or national money. In Nigeria, it is the *naira*. South Africa uses *rand*, Ghana uses *cedi*. United States uses *dollar,* and in the UK, it is *pound*.

Digital Currency
Digital money or currency is the existence of money in electronic form. The development of computer technology has allowed money to be represented

digitally. Money can now be stored in digital files on the internet in an electronic computer database by financial institutions.

Today, most money exists as digital money or in electronic form in the database of banks. Digital currencies exhibit properties similar to other currencies, but do not have a physical form of banknotes and coins. Not having a physical form, they allow for easier, faster, and more flexible payments.

Two examples of digital money are electronic money and crypto-currency. The former is issued and stored by financial institutions or banks while the latter runs on a decentralized control system, that is, it is not issued by a central authority. It is no news that crypto-currency is the latest innovation of what money can be in which *Bitcoin* is the most famous and widely acceptable of them all. As at the time of writing this book, there are over 6,000 cryptocurrencies.

Section Two

All that has been explained so far is not what money is, but all that money has been. Another form of money might evolve tomorrow; I can't tell, because the only limitation to innovation and discovery is death.

It is unwise to be pursuing what money can be without knowing what money truly is. The poor and middle-class only knows what money can be, so they chase after money, work for money, live for money, and eventually die without having the money. If you are going to be rich, you need to think like the rich. You need to reset your mind and refocus your energy on learning and doing what the rich do.

Personally, my existing opinions about money altered upon critical thinking and study of the rich. I realized the money lessons I learned from my parents were unbalanced and inconsistent with the present-day economy. They were not rich neither were they poor, the principle of money they sustained could only attain the middle-class level.

The middle-class level is grossly defined by academics. Get a good grade and you'll get a good pay. Be an "A Student" and first-class jobs will come looking for you, they tell me. Frankly speaking, even without job rewards, academics is a great venture but when looking for where to learn about money, academics is not the best option.

Many of us went to school with that money-making mindset only to graduate and find out that the rules are no longer what it used to be.

Were we disappointed? Oh yes!

We were really disappointed by those who made us believe so. Nevertheless, their actions are excusable because that is the degree to which they know about money in relation to academics (you truly can't give what you don't have).

If academics is going to aid your pursuit of money at all, it won't take you beyond the middle-class. From records, the rich guys out there rarely ever are academics. How many people ever became rich through bagging a professorial degree? The best school (academics) has done is to take you from the poor class to the middle-class level, but there is a class greater than that, and that is the class of the rich.

If you are going to advance to this level then you need to revamp yourself, change strategy, and adopt a new methodology. You need to stop learning from the poor and middle class, you need to start learning from the rich. The secret of money is with them that are rich.

Nobody has ever become rich by pursuing money. Chasing after money is not the game of the rich but the poor. It is like chasing all the pigs you see on the street because you saw a magician transformed into one. Meanwhile, a magician can take the form of anything he so wishes so is money. It can be anything.

The first secret I must tell you about money is that money is not real. The rich know this. So, chasing after it won't get you to it. Though, it appears real. Sooner, you'll realize what you are running after never truly exists because it is never enough no matter how much of it you think you have amassed or acquired.

The more you have it, the more it leaves you. The more you earn, the more you spend. The greater your income so would your expenses be. Unlike the rich, it is never so for them because they live by a different principle and their decisions in money-making are properly guided by it.

They are never afraid to invest even though the risk probability is high. They understand that the greater the risk, the greater the yield. For them, the game of money is, it is either you win or you lose. You either have or you don't. But the poor man doesn't think like that. He would do everything to protect the last dime on him because he thinks money is real.

Money and air share similar property. If you hold it, it vanishes. You keep it, it evaporates. How will money kept or saved evaporate, you ask? Do I also tell you that saving money is a bad idea? Well, in the course of this book you will know better.

The goal I'm set to achieve through this book is to teach you how the rich get rich and how the poor get poor.

This means anything I'm teaching you here are common practices of the rich and invariably, what the poor don't do that the rich do. There is a common saying, if you want to be rich then do what the rich do.

The rich don't live their lives working for money. They know chasing after more naira, more dollars, or pounds is not the way to wealth. They know money is not real. If money were to be real, why haven't hard work yielded the biggest reward?

Empirically, the greatest price for wealth should come through working hard, but sadly, it is not so. You wake up by 4 AM to go to work and return by 8 PM, yet you are not the richest man on your street. That's sixteen good hours you just spent working hard and by the end of the month when your salary comes, you're glad your hard work paid off after all. So, you are motivated to work harder every other month only to be paid what can be money.

What money can be cannot make you rich, only what money is can.

I read an article, some time ago, of an employee who congratulated his boss for buying a new car. The boss replied and said, "Thank you. I'll buy a better one next time if you work harder". That is rude and unethical, you say. At the same time, it is insanely true; you are paid to work for him. Moneywise, the one who paid you to work for or under him is financially smarter than you.

Now, here is wisdom. The one who paid you to earn for himself is wise, but the one who paid you to both earn and learn from you is wiser.

Practically, that is what your boss does. Logically, when employed, you are paid for your time, knowledge, experience, and also rewarded for your hard work by your boss. However, he stands at the gaining end because he is both earning and learning from you subconsciously. You do the greater work, he gets the greater share. You commit an error you get blamed. You do well, he gets praised. You work hard, he works smart.

Although, the reason you work "hard" in the first place is that you have a job made available to you by your boss and he pays you for the job. So you can never be greater than the one who pays you to earn because he is financially smarter than you. He built the systems and channels that birth your income. If you ever think hard work is what translates to money, then you are still far from having it. Who pays you to do your laundry, clean your house, read your books, and do some other personal stuff? Nobody!

Your boss in the office pays you for the same hard work, though in some other forms. The difference between these two is that the one you do for yourself is for yourself and is paid for by no one but the one you do for your boss is for others and is paid for by others, NOT your boss.

"It's not the employer who paid the wages. Employers only handle the money. It's the customer who paid the wages." **- Henry Ford**

You are only given a percentage of it as payment by your boss because he created the system through which the money flowed. So the boss is largely rewarded for the creation of the cashflow system than the employee who did the most work. What created that system is what I call *Idea.* Therefore, you must understand again, that money is not hard work, money is an idea. *This is the second secret of the rich and the realest definition of money.*

Does it occur to you that everything I earlier explained about what money can be was product of ideas? Starting from the oldest bartering system to the recent cryptocurrencies, you would realize that man transited from one form of money to another out of necessity. And necessity they say, is the mother of all invention and inventions are products of ideas. And ideas are created out of man's desire to solve a problem.

I described I-DE-A as "i-de-here". *I dey here* is a slang which translates to *I am here* in English. So, *idea* is all about choosing to be relevant in the face of problems. *The rich when looking for money create ideas. The poor when looking for money execute the ideas.*

No rich man, Jeff Bezos, Bill Gates, Aliko Dangote, and the host of others became great by chasing money. Rather, they sought a problem, created an idea, and built a system to solve it. That system is what translated into wealth. The rich knows money is not real, money is only an idea. No wonder Napoleon Hill said, *"Ideas are the beginning points of all fortunes."*

CHAPTER SUMMARY

- There is difference between what money is and what money can be.
- Money, in and of itself, is nothing; it derives its value by being a medium of exchange and a unit of measurement.
- Academics is a great venture but when looking for where to learn about money, academics is not the best option.
- The secret of money is with them that are rich.

- What money can be cannot make you rich, only what money is can.
- Money is not real. Money is an idea.
- The rich when looking for money creates ideas. The poor when looking for money executes the idea.

CHAPTER TWO

Owning Your Business

"Every problem is a gift - without problems we would not grow." –

Anthony Robbins

Before I completed my NYSC program, I got a job offer in Lagos, Nigeria to work as the acting Principal of a prestigious secondary school. The net worth of the school is over $100,000. It is a go-to-school for any parents that want a quality and productive academic career for their children.

My basic salary was to be $110 with minimum add-ons of $50, totaling $160 or more. Meanwhile, my employer was to wait for me to complete my one-year compulsory service to the nation, after which my service to his organization would resume immediately. At this juncture, you might be tempted to fault the recruitment policy of my boss or perhaps think this is some kind of family organization because I said my employer was to wait. How will a job be waiting for me in this era of widespread unemployment?

Actually, a job can wait for you if you are the only solution. Sentiments are only applicable in unqualified situations, not where proven records exist.

I was qualified for the job with proven records of results par excellence in that field. However, surprisingly, I declined the offer. Everyone thought I was out of my mind. You're probably thinking the same thing, right now. My family was most disappointed because they wanted to have me back in Lagos, especially with the security situation in the North.

It seemed like a good opportunity to return to the West and start my life as a fresh graduate with a good job offer and a leadership role. Nevertheless, I stood by my decision. Sincerely, it wasn't easy to say no. You know it is always easier to buy fish from the market than approaching the river with your hook and net especially when you have a phobia for water.

Dealing with the Phobia

I'm sure you know I wouldn't have declined that opportunity if I had no plan B. The quality of our decision is always a product of the information available. That is what we call informed decisions. Although that offer was considerably nice, I saw something bigger than just satisfying an immediate need. Delayed gratification is always an investment with huge dividends going forward. So, sometimes it pays not to jump at every reward for diligence not because you don't deserve it but because it is capable of impeding your vision to strive for greater laurels.

After I completed my NYSC program in Nasarawa State, North-Central, Nigeria, the persuasion from my family to return to Lagos persisted and my employer's reception continued as he was calling from time to time to convince me otherwise. The pressure to return home and accept the job offer continued. Meanwhile, in the course of service, I had foreseen the prospect of a particular business that I was saving towards. By the time my service was over I had saved about $300 coupled with grants from friends and family, I had over $500 to start the business.

Having capital is not the same as starting a business. If capital is all that it takes to establish a business, then banks wouldn't be giving loans to businessmen and no one would be saving money in the bank either, everyone would probably have turned a CEO. So, it is one thing to have a capital, it is another thing to eventually start. The truth is, there is always the presence of fear when you are about to start any business; the fear of not believing in yourself, fear of loss of money, fear of competition, and oppression. These phobias are necessary and are only stumbling blocks to prove whether you're up to the tasks.

I must tell you this; the beginning stage of a business is not always easy. However, you must know why you're into it in the first place and believe in yourself.

The factors involved in starting a business vary depending on the business type. However, three major factors hold true for all businesses. The factors are mindset, skill or expertise, and capital. Other factors may include location, competition, manpower, logistics, et cetera.

For an entrepreneur or one who is willing to go into business, if any of these major factors is lacking, particularly the mindset factor, then that business is automatically a failed one even before it begins. The mind is everything in life. Your personality, family, business, and everything around you is a reflection of your mind. The success or failure of your business is also determined by the mind. So, the first thing you need as a business starter is the right mind. Yes, having the right mind is the first step because many negative thoughts would run through your mind that you would not be able to give answers to, and anything you can't give an answer to becomes your fear. If you want to go into importation business for instance; the questions pertaining to the risk involved can culminate into fear.

You could be asking questions like; how can I guarantee the originality of the goods? Hope the goods won't crash in the air or capsize on the sea? If it arrives, hope thieves won't burgle my shop and cart away with the goods? These are very important questions to the success of that business, but I will advise that the ones you can answer please answer, and ones you can't, just have the right mindset.

Also, trust your skills and believe in yourself; you don't know how good you are or can be if you don't try. With every trial come a new knowledge, a different approach and a greater drive to succeed. Practice enhances perfection. Hence, to gain mastery over your phobia is to have the right mindset, believe in yourself, trust your skills, raise your capital and start. Yes, START THAT BUSINESS!

Dealing with the People
The next thing I want to tell you about starting a business might distort your pre-existing business knowledge but if understood and appropriately applied, it would set you on course as a multi-preneur. Therefore, you must be willing to learn, unlearn, and relearn.

You've often heard that the first thing you need to start a business is an idea. Well, that is not totally true. The first thing you need is "People." It is like telling a driver that the first thing he needs to convey you to a location is fuel. The first thing he needs is not fuel but a vehicle. The function of the fuel is to power the engine of the vehicle. So, fuel is useless where there are no engines because the fuel cannot work by itself. Similarly, an idea by itself cannot produce anything unless it finds the right people.

There are different fuels for different engines. The fuel that runs an aeroplane is not the same that is used to power a car. The fact that a business idea was successful in Canada doesn't mean it will succeed in China. The people and the environment are not the same. Different strokes for different folks. Selling a food item that is native to Igbos in northern Nigeria, you obviously won't sell. So, it is possible to have a good business idea and be in the wrong market.

Another reason you should prioritize people above idea is that the money you are looking for is with the people. Invariably, the larger the people you solve their problems the richer you are. Don't forget this, no money without people.

People and their problems are the first consideration in generating a business idea or creating a business plan.

Where people abound, opportunities for wealth is endless. No wonder you hear slogan like "there is money in Lagos." So, when you find a people the next thing is to find an idea that can run within that system. Just as fuel is designed to operate an engine, so is an idea used to monetize a people.

Consider this; to buy anything you would need money but what is it that buys money – idea. Sell an idea to people and you would buy their money from them. That is what the rich do.

Don't forget this, the reason the rich is rich and the poor is poor is because the rich pay you but the society pays the rich. Until the society (people) pay you, you may not be rich and the way the society can pay you is through owning your business. *This is the third secret of the rich.*

Dealing with your product
After you have overcome the phobia and have found people, the next thing is to develop a product. Before that, you must discover a need or problem that exists amongst the people. I prefer using the word *problem* and not *need* because it is more persuasive. You would agree with me that not all needs must be met but all problems require a solution.

In starting a business, don't just make a choice because you like the business or it is clean, lucrative and your friends are into it. The real thing you should look out for is, does it address a major problem? How rich you would get is determined by how big the problem you solve.

Let me give you a relatable instance. Some months back, a global problem struck the world. For the first time in a long time, the rich and the poor, small and great, virtually every man had the same problem "the fear of Corona Virus."

Before the outbreak, according to Forbes, the richest man in the world is Jeff Bezos. Nature perhaps wanting to change the economic status quo opened an opportunity to any man who would find the cure, vaccine or solution to the pandemic and develop a product for it. Let's say it is to be sold for $100/one. That's about $800 billion if the whole world is to be vaccinated. See how another man would have climbed up the ladder of the world's richest man because he had a solution to a global problem.

So, true wealth is by discovering a problem and developing a product to solve it; the problem determines the product.

As I bring this chapter to a close, I have just given you the three steps (3Ps) that guided me into becoming a business owner today. I overcame the *Phobia*, found *People*, and developed a *Product* that serves them best.

Honestly, I am yet to understand why people commit the best part of their lives in managing another man's business while if they invest the same in their personal businesses, it would probably be close to succeeding now.

The prospect of my $500 business is worth more than a million naira today. Rather than manage the business of another; I chose to manage mine. Rather than sit in the office, I chose the field because real money experience is in the field. I'm not discouraging anyone from working under a boss. My point is simple, *working under someone is but a time of life employment; working for yourself is a lifetime investment.*

CHAPTER SUMMARY

- To deal with business phobia - have the right mindset, trust your skills, raise your capital and then START.

- The first thing you need to start a business is not an idea but people; idea comes next.

- People and their problems are the first consideration in generating a business idea or creating a business plan.

- Sell an idea to people and you would buy their money from them.

- True wealth is by discovering a problem and developing a product to solve it; the problem determines the product.

- Working under someone is but a time of life employment but working for yourself is a lifetime investment.

PART TWO

KEEPING YOUR MONEY

CHAPTER THREE

Invest to Harvest

"So long the earth remains, seedtime and harvest will not cease."

Genesis 8:22

The universal saying goes, "what you sow, you will reap." In other words, "what you invest, you will harvest." It may only take time, but it will certainly happen. Time is the defining factor for growth and any change in event.

Time is the line that separates the sowing period from the harvest. For an infant to grow and become an adult, it requires time. Your efforts in the field of practice, studying, and working hard requires time before it's been rewarded. Your devotion to reading this book also requires time. Indeed, time management is fundamental to personal improvement. Whether you will be rich or poor, is largely dependent on what you do with your time. Needless to say, your first and greatest investment is in the wise usage of time.

Now let's talk about investment. The term *investment* can refer to any mechanism used for generating future income.

Generally, investment is a deliberate act of an individual that involves the deployment of money, time, or effort in securities, assets, knowledge, or skill acquisition with a view to obtaining returns over a specified period of time. In an economic sense, an investment is the purchase of goods that are not consumed today but are used in the future to create wealth. In finance, an investment is a monetary asset purchased with the idea that the asset will provide income in the future or will later be sold at a higher price for a profit.

Summarily, investment is making your money work for you. This is the fourth secret of the rich.

The rich are good investors. They don't work for money instead money works for them. Unlike the poor who works because he needs money. Since he feels that the greater the work the bigger the income, so he works a little more and a little more. Although, it is true that work brings money. However, by strength, you can't work all the works required to earn you money enough to sustain you a lifetime, for times are coming when the strength to work would no longer be available. So, it becomes imperative that you become wise about the dealings of life and in your use of money.

God through nature has taught man several lessons that are key to wealth multiplication through investment. The first lesson was He gave us the earth (ground) that requires a seed in which over a period of time, the seeds germinate, grows, and reproduces itself in large quantity.

Secondly, the Bible told us that on the seventh day, God rested from all His works. So, God is no longer in the business of creating man and stuff. However, man keeps increasing by the day. How possible is that? After He made the first man and the first woman, he created a system of reproduction within them. To the man, He gave sperm and the woman an ovum or egg cell. Biologically, we were told that as these reproductive systems interact, it results in the fertilization of the woman's ovum by the man's sperm resulting into another life called embryo in the woman's womb. After nine months, this embryo develops into a full baby and a new life is delivered. Lest I forget, the man's sperm was another seed that took a period of nine months to mature.

So, God does not have to actively create another man. As long as the earth remains, and it is inhabited by a man and woman in their right frame of mind, reproduction would never cease. That is yet another great investment.

The greatest of them all, is in the fact that God invested Himself to have the world, not just the Jews, but the world. Yes, that's the biggest investment of all times.

So you must learn this principle that to have is to put in, to harvest is to invest, nothing comes out of nothing, and the bigger your investment the greater your harvest.

The rich know this that, nothing in nature reproduces itself without a programmable or conscious effort put into its design during production. Anything that reproduces itself by itself is a weed and not a seed. Money is to be consciously grown using the right formula. When it is not, it doesn't stay. This is why the poor, amongst many other reasons, don't have it because they have not learned the art of growing it.

Money in the hand of the poor is a weed, they consume it. Money in the hand of the rich is a seed, they sow it.

When the poor possess money, he sets fire on it, destroys it, and tomorrow he comes looking for another like a weed smoker. On the other hand, the rich gather it, sow it, grow it, tender it, and boom, it multiplies. If you want to accurately measure the wealth of the rich, go to their field of investment. There is no rich man who is not an investor. He may not have started out to be one during his humble beginnings however, in the course of growing his business and gaining a steady flow of income, investment would surely have been a key player.

Bill Gates has over 60% of his wealth invested in stocks. Warren Buffett who is widely regarded as the most successful investor in the world began his journey to wealth with $174,000. Today, he is worth over $50,000,000,000. Jeff Bezos, currently the richest man in the world, invested $250,000 in Google stock in 1998. Today, that money is worth over $3Billion. That is only 2.1% of his total net worth of about $140,000,000,000. If you are ever going to get rich, then you must do what the rich do, they invest in assets.

The fifth secret of the rich is that they buy assets and not liability.

Robert Kiyosaki in his book "Rich Dad Poor Dad" defined assets as what puts money into your pocket, and liability as what takes money away from you.

The rich put their money to work by investing in assets. The poor put their money to death by accumulating liabilities.

When expenses are more than income, how do you expect to have a reserve? When your liabilities are more than your assets, how can you have a seed to sow? The rich know this, that seed is important to the sustainability of their wealth so they keep increasing their asset column.

They are two types of assets; real assets and financial assets. Real assets are tangible assets used to produce goods or services, such as buildings, machinery, and landed property. They can also be cognitive assets that are utilized in the production of commodities or services such as intellectual property. While financial assets on the other hand are claims on real assets or income produced by real assets. Examples include stocks and bonds which, on their own, are worthless papers and do not directly contribute to the production of a commodity or service but derive their value from the claims they carry.

Friends, I encourage you, to climb the ladder of the rich, start investing in assets. Buy landed properties, get involved in real estate, buy stocks, find a financial adviser to guide you through profitable markets. Invest your seeds in values that appreciate over time and this includes gold and silver. We don't have too many of them but their values cannot be over-emphasized. They are scarce commodities, and a scarce commodity is an expensive commodity therefore, it is worth an investment. Don't forget the general rule of successful investing – buy when everyone else is selling and hold until everyone else is buying.

In preparing your seed for investment, here are some factors to consider:

1. Risk Reward Ratio

Any kind of investment would involve a certain degree of risk. What's important is that you take on calculated risk and stick to a risk/reward ratio that suits your risk appetite. A risk reward ratio compares the expected returns of an investment to the amount of risk undertaken to invest in that asset.

This ratio is calculated by dividing the amount the investor stands to lose (risk) if the price moves in the unexpected direction by the amount of profit (reward) one expects to have made when the investment is successful.

For example, you put in $100 into an investment that offers to pay you $400 as return in the not-so-distant future. If the deal is successful, your profit is $300. The risk reward ratio is calculated as $100:$300, that is, 1:3. So, you risked $100 to make $300. This is quite rewarding.

If the investment offers to pay you $200. The risk reward ratio will be 1:1. Risking $100 to gain $100 is not an ideal investment unless no risk is involved. For most investors, 1:2 is considered the minimum. However, you have to decide for yourself what the acceptable ratio is for you.

2. Investment Capital

The next thing to consider is your investment capital as it largely affects your choice of investment. I hear some people with good business ideas say they don't have capital to start up. Your business idea is not complete until it is able to source the capital to drive it.

Capital is the amount of money required to fund a business or investment. Usually, the higher the capital, the higher the profit margin. This is so because there is a clear difference between what you can invest in with $5,000 compared to $100,000. However, this does not limit your chances of success as you can leverage loans from banks, individuals, or other financial institutions for financial support and to give you the boost you need as a starter.

In fact, taking a loan is a rather common practice by investors since most of us will not be able to pay down the entire amount needed to start a business. Only be sure the risk reward ratio is highly favourable and not incur unnecessary debts.

3. Time

Every investment needs time to yield. Time is a very important factor in considering investment options.

While some investments take days to cash-out, some may last for years before it yields the expected return. Usually, the shorter the time horizon the less risky the investment but the bigger the interest and the longer the time horizon the riskier the investment but the greater the interest.

One way to manage the risks of investment is having sound background knowledge of the commodity before investing your money as this helps to guide how long you commit yourself to the deal and when it's most appropriate to cash out. With good knowledge of an investment, you are able to determine the right time to sow and the best time to reap. Poor decision making owing to ignorance has made many investors lose a great deal during volatile periods of an investment.

Last year, I invested $450 into melon storage program with the hope that the price would rise some months later thus, making $500 or more as profit. After six months, due to the uncertainty of the market, the price, instead of rising declined so low to a loss of about 70% of my capital. I, having the knowledge of the time duration my commodity can span; I decided to hoard it for another year if perhaps the price would pick. Fortunately, it did.

Two major things the rich invest in:

1. **Knowledge and Concept**

Another thing the rich invests in is knowledge. All you're learning about investment will be useless if you lack the fundamental principle of how it works. Being told what will help you might not help you until you know how. The "how question" is important to making the best choices in life because it is the road map to desired destination. When we don't know where we are going so we inquire.

Inquiry creates an imaginative perspective of the possibility of your destination. Many have failed financially on the path to wealth because they don't know how to arrive there and they don't seek knowledge. Knowledge, most often than not comes through inquiry. When inquiry is activated, there is the will to research. When we research, we find answers that give birth to solutions.

The rich don't invest their money in what they have little or no knowledge about. They rather pay to acquire the knowledge than pay for loss brought about by ignorance. Although, loss is not a loss in the real sense if you acquire the lessons. However, too many losses might mean you don't know the rules of the game. So before you play the game, know the rules.

You want to invest in landed properties, read books on Real Estate Management. You want to buy shares and stocks, get a credible and successful stoke broker to school you on that. If yours is in real money such as gold and silver or forex trade, find an expert in that field. Whatever you want to invest in, seek knowledge in that area.

The success and profitability of an investment is preconditioned upon understanding the fundamental working principle of its concept. Let me give you this illustration. A man sowed a seed because he saw others doing so. When the seed grew and bore fruits he was amazed at his harvest. So he decided to sow more seeds for bigger harvest. Unknowingly to him, the rainy season was over, and all his investments perished. What this man lacked is concept.

Understanding concept is essential to succeeding in any investment. Concept is the A-Z of investment. It teaches you when to invest and when not to. With concept, you know the conditions that favor an investment, such that if the conditions are not palatable, you create it. From the analogy I gave above, that man didn't know the success of his seed is premised upon water. When the natural water stopped, had he known he would have created an artificial water system, that is, irrigation. That is, understanding concept.

Don't put your money into an investment because everyone is doing so. That will be a very stupid reason. Understand its concept before you do so. With concept, you have control. *The rich control the market and issue more receipts to the poor because they have concepts.* Let your investment policy be guided by knowledge and the power of concept.

Benjamin Franklin once said, *"an investment in knowledge pays the best interest."* You know why? It is because with knowledge and concept, you are in charge.

2.   People

The rich invest in people. Investing in people is the most important and perhaps the greatest of all investments. Even God invested His Son into the world and gained the world. Every other investment dies with you except the one you invest in people. The only investment that outlives you is your seeds (good memories) in the heart of others.

Where are the remains of the richest men of old today? Who still remembers the wealth of M.K.O Abiola, Alexander the Great, Mansa Musa or Muammar Gaddafi? Unlike John D. Rockefeller, Andrew Carnegie and Henry Ford whose wealth transit time. These men invested in people and so their legacy lives on. The quality and longevity of your business is determined by your workers.

As a business man, invest in your workers. As a leader, invest in your followers. As a pastor, invest in your members. Anything that will be great and stand the test of time needs people. The real measure of your wealth is how much you'd be worth if you lost all your money.

My pastor, Daddy E.A Adeboye, in one of his sermons said, some judge wealth by monetary value but true wealth is investing in people because if the richest man in the world wants to buy a tie, he takes out money from his pocket to do so. However, if he (speaking about himself) wants a tie, he only needs to say it and millions of ties would appear without taking a dime from his pocket. So judge, who then is the richest? True riches come by making others rich.

Notable philanthropist of our time, Bill Gates, according to Forbes has contributed over $34,000,000,000 of his wealth to charity organizations. When your wealth has no positive impact on people, it is useless.

As important as money is, all the money in the world is not sufficient to buy just one person. People gave value to money not the other way. No one is rich in isolation. In other words, none can be rich without people, for riches are made from people. *Material assets cannot keep your legacy forever only human asset has the capacity to do so.*

Here are the words of **Michael Steinhardt,** one of life's greatest investors to help you stay grounded and successful in your business and field of investment:

- *Make all of your mistakes early in life. The more tough lessons early on, the fewer errors you make later.*

- *Always make your living doing something you enjoy.*

- *Be intellectually competitive. The key to research is to assimilate as much data as possible in order to be to the first to sense a major change.*

- *Make good decisions even with incomplete information. You will never have all the information you need. What matters is what you do with the information you have.*

- *Always trust your intuition, which resembles a hidden supercomputer in the mind. It can help you do the right thing at the right time if you give it a chance.*

- *Don't make small investments. If you're going to put money at risk, make sure the reward is high enough to justify the time and effort you put into the investment decision.*

CHAPTER SUMMARY

- Investment is making your money work for you.

- To have is to put in, to harvest is to invest, nothing comes out of nothing.
- Money in the hand of the poor is a weed, they consume it. But money in the hand of the rich is a seed, they sow it.
- Buy assets not liabilities.
- You need to have the knowledge and understand the concept on which your business or investment thrives.
- Invest in people; the quality and longevity of your business is determined by your workers.

PART THREE

GROWING YOUR MONEY

CHAPTER FOUR

Don't Spend Money, Send Money

"To him that has, more will be given and he will have abundance; but to him that doesn't have even the little he has will be taken away from him."

Matthew 25:29

"Adams, it's so generous of your dad to have left you with such a sum, indeed he was a good man," said Uncle Joe.

"Yes he was, and I miss him greatly, particularly his financial wisdom. I'm still astounded about how he turned few dollars to streams of income, as I read from his biography." Adams replied.

"Yes, he had a humble beginning but an enviable end. So sad he left you too soon. They say, a good man leaves an inheritance for his children but a great man passes the heritage. Been the great man he was, I'm sure he not only left you this large sum but also passed to you the secret to his financial freedom." Uncle Joe asked.

"No, Uncle Joe and that is why I have come to see you if you could guide me on the path to riches." Adams responded.

"But you're already rich what else do you desire?" asked Uncle Joe.

"This is my father's wealth not mine. Unless I learn the laws of money the spirit that controls money will not be happy with me and all that my father worked for would vanish into the thin air and there would be nothing to pass on to my children." Adams replied.

"You have actually spoken like a wise son. In deed all that your father lived to acquire can be gone in day if you fail to understudy the secrets of money." Uncle Joe responded.

"There's a secret I'm going to teach you, it's the secret to making money, keeping money and growing money. I call it The Seven Secrets of the Rich." Uncle Joe added.

"Are you ready to learn these secrets?"

"Sure!" replied Adams.

"The first of these seven secrets is that money is not real. Sadly, not many know this; often when we run short of money, we begin to blame ourselves that we've not worked hard enough then we result to working harder or staying on multiple jobs to solve our money problems. We've been made to believe that it's through chasing money we make money but that's not true. Oftentimes, the money we make through chasing is soon blown away by the wind of necessity and we return to our initial state of want. Note this; until your income outweighs your necessity, wealth is far from you. Usually, the money we chase to have disappears through spending while the one created through an idea is so sufficient that it abides through investment saving."

"This brings us to the second secret which is, money is an idea. Contrary to popular opinion, the first thing you need to make money is not money but an idea. In fact, you can make money without spending money but it's impossible to run a money producing system without financial ideas.

An idea is a mind conception that proffers imaginative solutions to real life problems, but financial ideas offers solutions to money problems. Most importantly, it helps you to monetize economic problems. Engaging your ideas to solving economic problems through self-enterprise (entrepreneurship) is the beginning process on your journey to wealth. The more problems your ideas solve the more money you make because it is the successful implementation of your ideas that in-turn generate money."

"The third secret of the rich is that you own your own business. The richest man in the world today owns a business. The poorest man in the world has no business. Those in the middle class probably work for someone. You can't be rich spending all your years working for someone when will you start working for yourself? You need to work for yourself before money can work for you. And until money begins to work for you, you can't make money."

"The fourth secret of the rich is you need to make your money work for you. While the average man only employs fellow men, animals and machines to work for him. The rich are a step ahead; they employ money as well. In fact, money is their biggest employee because they have learnt the act of making money work for them. They know how to command money and make it do their biddings. They control money while the poor and middle class is controlled by money. This is why the poor and middle class work for the rich."

"This brings us to the fifth secret which is, the rich buy assets not liability. I told you the fourth secret is to make your money work for you, but how do you make your money work for you? You make your money work for you through investments, that is, by buying assets and not liabilities. Store your money in valuables that appreciate overtime like landed properties, stocks, gold and crypto-currencies. Any commodity that is capable of returning the future value of your   money higher than you bought it is an asset. Go for it. Invest your money in assets and not liability."

"Dear Adams, I have shown you how to make money and keep it. To make money, learn the first 3 secrets. To keep money, learn secrets 4 and 5." Uncle Joe added.

"Thanks Uncle Joe for the financial education. This is a treasure for me; I'll make sure I keep it as I will need it on my journey to wealth". Adams said.

"But Sir, I have one more request" Adams continued.

"Go ahead" replied, Uncle Joe.

"Please Uncle, can you teach me how to spend the money my father willed to me?" asked Adams

"Spend the money, you say, ok! But maybe we should hear how an average man spends money" replied Uncle Joe.

Uncle Roberts calls out to Phil his secretary.

"Phil, if you were given $500,000. How would you spend it?" Uncle Roberts asked.

"$500,000 wow! That's huge. Well, for me, my rent would soon be due and my landlord has been acting like a bug lately. So firstly, I'll use 70% to buy a land and build a house of my choice on it. Secondly, I've been spending too much on transportation as my current car is bad; engine today, battery tomorrow. It's sickening. Therefore, 20% will go for a new car as it covers for undue visit to the mechanic workshop and excessive transport fares and would also be nice on a new house. While the remaining part will be kept for uncertainties. Phil concluded.

"Thank you Phil, you may go on with your work" said, Uncle Joe.

Looking at Adams, he continued. "Did you hear how an average man thinks about money, what do you think about his response?"

"Hmm, I think he was more focused on using the money to meet his immediate needs without future investments. Those needs, according to what you initially taught me are liabilities and not assets" replied, Adams.

"Very good, son! Now you see the poor is poor because he has little or no knowledge about financial wisdom. A dull financial mind cannot exude financial greatness." Uncle Joe added.

"But do I condemn his ideas, no; the quality of our decisions is but a function of our knowledge. Sound knowledge is what helps us to effectively manage and transform our haves to produce our needs."

Ecclesiastes 10:10

"If the axe is dull, and one does not sharpen the edge, then much strength is engaged; but wisdom brings success."

"Knowing how to rightfully apply what you have is essential to financial success. When you see a poor man check how he manages what he has compared to the rich, that quality of knowledge in the rich to transform what he has to meet his needs is the reason for his wealth." Uncle Joe, continued.

"One more difference between the poor and the rich again is, the poor, when faced with a problem looks for what is made, while the rich looks for what he can make."

"When we are in need, we are not supposed to look outside but within, for within us is the raw material needed to manufacture the end product of our wants.

Everything in the open was made from something hidden." Uncle Joe added.

"Hmmm! So true" replied Adams.

"His knowledge as expressed in his plans only reflects his desire to solve a recurring problem with a short term solution", continued, Uncle Joe.

"It is good he wanted to build a house and buy a car; they are both basic necessities of a normal life. However, owning these things do not permanently fix his housing and transportation needs. I understand it relieves of some expenses but only for a while because, one can't live in a house for 50years without fixes and renovations neither can one ride one car for the rest of his life without having to change parts." Uncle Joe added.

"But there's nothing that one buys or acquires that doesn't require maintenance, what's important is the comfort and satisfaction derived", retorted Adams.

"Comfort with more expenses and comfort with more income, which is better?" Uncle Joe asked.

"Comfort with income", replied Adams.

"To enjoy comfort with income you must learn how to save for the future". Uncle Joe said

"How does one save for the future?" asked Adams.

"It is by sending today's money on errand". Uncle Joe replied.

"But how possible is that?" Adams asked

"Do you know the rich don't spend money instead they send money. Wonder why the rich are the highest spenders yet the money doesn't seem to depart from them? It is because they send money they don't spend money." Uncle Joe said.

"You don't spend money?" Adams asked …….. "You mean you don't buy stuffs, then how did you acquire this?" pointing at Uncle Joe's suit.

Smiles, "I acquired it, not by spending money but by sending money" Uncle Joe replied.

 "What do you mean by sending money" asked Adams.

"Sending money is the act of spending money without losing money. This is the sixth secret of the rich. What you spend leaves you but what you send returns to you. Money is your messenger, send it on errand and make it work for you. This is how the rich get richer; they don't spend money, they send money. When they spend or buy to pay, a repayment plan has already been initiated, so they acquire and keep acquiring without losing money."

"See why a portion of the Bible says, *To him that has, more will be given and to him that doesn't have even the little he has will be taken away from him.*""

"I learnt this principle in my late twenties; ever since then, for every penny that left me, I'd already created a system in my mind to regain it if not double it. And it has always worked." Uncle Joe, concluded.

"Wow! This is an eye-opener, Sir."

"This is very sound financial wisdom. Thank you Uncle Joe." Adams replied.

CHAPTER SUMMARY

- Chasing money can't get you to wealth.
- Engaging your ideas to solving economic problems through self enterprise (entrepreneurship) is the beginning process on your journey to wealth.
- While the average man only employs fellow men, animals and machines to work for him. The rich are a step ahead; they employ money as well to work for them.
- The poor, when faced with a problem looks for what is made, while the rich, when faced with a problem looks for what he can make.

- Sending money is the act of spending money without losing money.

CHAPTER FIVE

Time Monetization

"Time is the coin of your life. It is the only coin you have, and only you can determine how it will be spent. Be careful lest you let other people spend it for you." - Carl Sandburg

Now, let me teach you the second way to grow money.

This is the seventh secret of the rich

"Are you ready?" asked Uncle Joe.

"Yes sir!" replied Adams.

"Have you ever asked your dad to tell you the secrets to his wealth?" Uncle Joe asked.

 "Yes, couple of times, but he kept making promises that he would make out time for me. The last time we spoke about it he was so sure that our next appointment will not be compromised then the unfortunate event happened" replied Adams.

Hmmm!

"Do you think his failure to fulfill his promise was due to his unwillingness to tell you the secret?" asked Uncle Joe.

"No sir, I think he was just too busy" replied Adams.

"Yes, he was too busy making money with his time." Uncle Joe responded swiftly.

"One major secret to your dad's wealth is in his ability to convert time to money. You must have often heard people say time is money. What that implies is that, if you have time you can have money provided you know how to monetize it. Benjamin Franklin said, *"Time is money. Waste it now. Pay for it later!"* Uncle Joe added.

"To be rich you must learn how to buy time and monetize it this is the seventh secret of the rich.

One way to grow your money is to learn the act of buying time. Amongst all assets, time is the greatest and the most valuable so, of all investments, investment in time is the greatest. The poor, rich and middle class all know how to invest in material assets, but the reason the rich is always ahead is because they invest in time; they buy and sell time. They know how to buy your time for less and make the society pay hugely for their time. Time monetization is a common practice amongst rich; they use their money to lure you to sell your time cheaply to them but trade theirs for a huge fee thus, making more money. The rich are good in making the poor spend their time on them.

Carl Sandburg said, *"Time is the coin of your life. It is the only coin you have, and only you can determine how it will be spent. Be careful lest you let other people spend it for you."*" Uncle Joe continued.

"Another major difference between the poor and the rich is what they do with their time. The poor engages all his strength to do a task but the rich employs workers and pay for their time while he uses that same time for something more productive and rewarding than the wages he just paid his workers."

"To grow your money you need to learn the act of buying time. Increment in wealth is determined by the number of people in your income list. The higher the number, the greater the income, this is why the rich keeps getting richer because he is being paid by the people. Unlike the poor who is paid by one man; his boss. You cannot be rich when you're paid just by one person no matter how rich the individual is. If you keep selling your time to him without you buying time in return to compensate for your sold time, you stand at loss because before you know, retirement age would set in and there won't be energy to effectively maximize time in old age. So, be ready to buy time from whoever is willing to sell to you. Only know how to put the time into productive use. You'll be twice richer than keeping the money and spending your own time on the task." Uncle Joe added.

"I earlier said the rich is paid by the people. Oh, yes! The community, state, country, even the world pays them; that is why their wealth keeps increasing."

"And how do they get people to pay them? They do so by buying time from the poor to increase their productivity and market presence thereby earn a large database of payers as customers. The bigger your market, the higher the number of people that pays you hence, the higher your cash-flow. Jeff Bezos, Bill Gates, Aliko Dangote, and others are all time buyers. Consider the number of people they are paying to work for them you would realize they are rich because they have the largest bank of time." Uncle Joe responded.

"Hmm, the one that has the largest bank of time should invariably have the largest bank of money", Adams mused thoughtfully.

"Exactly son, that's the point!" Uncle Joe retorted.

"So, finally Adams, besides buying time from people; buy time for your health. Rest when you're supposed to, eat when you're hungry. Do exercise and go for regular medical check-ups. Again, buy time for your family; they come first in everything. Also buy time for your mental fitness. Read books. Pay for that seminar that a 5-year work experience may not give you. Above all, buy time for your Creator; this is very important because He owns the times." Uncle Joe concluded.

"Wow!"

"Your words are so powerful. You are awe-inspiring Sir. You practically changed my financial DNA. I don't know how to thank you." said Adams.

"When your wealth surpasses your father's, then you've thanked me." Uncle Joe replied.

"This is the most important moment of my life. Nobody has ever taught me about money like you did. I literally feel like the richest man in the world right now."

"Really, but for now, you are only the richest man in your family." Uncle Joe said jokingly.

They both laughed.

CHAPTER SUMMARY

- If you have time you can have money provided you know how to monetize it.
- Amongst all assets, time is the greatest and the most valuable so, of all investments, investment in time is the greatest.
- Increment in wealth is determined by the number of people in your income list.
- The bigger your market, the higher the number of people that pay you hence, the higher your cashflow.
- The rich are rich because they have the largest bank of time.

CHAPTER SIX

Final Words

There is a common saying that the most important words of a man are his last words. Many books including this have attempted to show us the secrets to wealth using different methodology but *I present to you the surest roadmap to wealth is doing what the rich do.*

To replicate the result of another is by doing exactly what he did. If you want to be rich, carefully study the rich, repeat their pattern and you will replicate their result. Though it may be cumbersome to study every rich man and woman alive as their path to wealth vary from person to person.

Different individual may have adopted different rules, principles or methodology in their journey to wealth as summarized in this book. However, through research, I have come to find out one habit is common to them all – the habit of investing. The rich have money and control money because of their investment ideology.

Majority today still think that the best way to have money is by saving money. This is a childhood mentality we grew up to adopt as it was the culture then when we were children. In those days, our parents in order to teach us how to save got us a 'safe' that is, a small rectangular wooden box, although some children that couldn't resist the temptation of snacks used the iron version so as to guide against the urge to break the box. This was the culture in many homes, and we were happy as kids doing it because it became a competition, as we tend to challenge our friends about how much we have saved, so it was fun.

Honestly, the excitement that comes with the fact that as a kid, you were able to have a particular amount of money to yourself (though small but huge compared to other kids) was overwhelming.

However, the drawback of this beautiful childhood financial experience is that it has little or no application in adulthood. That system of money growth dies at childhood, since it is only obtainable in situations where you don't work for money (what you don't work for you don't know the value) and are not saddled with responsibilities, which is the typical case scenario of childhood; no responsibilities, no expenses. So the money just keeps adding up. A child who saves $10 per day since he was born would have saved Thirty-six thousand and five hundred dollars ($36,500) by the time he turns 10 years.

That's a good deal I would say however, the fluidity of money doesn't permit for the application of saving money to grow money in adulthood. Unfortunately, many adults are yet to outgrow this system, we still save money in our homes, in advanced safe boxes, which is today's bank and also commit to mutual funding (co-operatives) with the aim of growing money meanwhile, the rules have changed.

Money Value Reduces through Saving

Money doesn't grow in safes, cooperatives or banks. You don't grow money by keeping or saving it; keeping money to grow it rather decreases it value. The purchasing power of money (national currency) usually reduces with time due to inflation. Inflation is when the purchasing power of money decreases.

For example, you save $1000/month in the bank, this would accumulate to $24,000 over 24 months but the worth of $10,000 2years ago might just be the same as $24,000 today. That is, goods $24,000 can buy now might just be the same as what $10,000 could buy 2 years ago and values $100 could buy 5 years ago is not the same value you will get for that same amount now. So, we see again that the value of money is dependent on time because the value depreciates with time. Therefore, saving money is not a habit of the rich.

Even in the Bible, God expressed displeasure towards the servant who saved his talent instead of trading with it to gain more. Whatsoever we have has a seed nature of multiplying itself if only we'll but invest it.

Saving and Investment

I know you'd say nobody saves money forever; most people do so with the intent to meet a future need or raise a capital for investment. Well, that may be true but rather than commit your money to mutual funding or banks to grow it, let me teach you what the rich does.

Say you want to save $10,000 over 10months that means you must commit $1,000 to savings per month. Assuming you got the first $1,000 and you commit it to a business or an investment whose ROI was $300 per month. Over 10months you would have made $3,000. That is, 30% profit of your initial capital. If you keep committing $1,000 into the investment every other month at the same interest rate, by the end of the tenth month, you would have made $16,500 as profit with your $10,000 savings intact whereas saving your money in the bank or through mutual funding (cooperative) only returns to you the actual amount saved and probably at a reduced value due to inflation.

I was reading through one of Aliko Dangote's articles where he stated that, one of the policies of his company is that they don't save money in banks instead they invest it. Warren Buffet, one of the richest men in the world is regarded as the biggest investor of all time. The richest men of our time, Jeff Bezos, Bill Gates, Jack Ma, Donald Trump, Robert Kiyosaki to mention but few are all big time investors.

If you want to be rich you must learn the habits of the rich. Investing is the culture of the rich, saving is the culture of the poor and middle class. You can't be doing what the poor do and expects to be rich that would defy the universal law of harvest – what you sow, you'll reap.

One good thing investing does for you is that, it makes your money works for you contrary to the general believe of you working for money. Until you begin to make your money work for you, wealth may be far from you. There's no amount of work you can do that can get you to wealth if you lack this financial intelligence. One day work will stop, whether by retirement or job loss. Whichever way it comes, the impact is the same – bankruptcy.

If you'd always have to work before you earn you're yet to be financially free. The apex of financial freedom is to build a system of cashflow such that whether you work or not, money doesn't cease to flow to you. The wealth of the rich is not determined by their work but by a system called – CASHFLOW. This is the secret to sustaining wealth.

Finally, I hereby encourage you to apply all the lessons on money you've come to know in this book. If you do, I'm confident that we'll meet on the other side of wealth.

Thank you for reading.

I wish to know how this book has helped you. Please, feel free to share your experiences.

God bless you.

You can connect with me via:

E-mail: laurensam24@gmail.com

Facebook: facebook.com/laurenz.sam24

LinkedIn: linkedin/samuel-g-lawrence

Twitter: @samylaurence

APPENDIX

RICH	MIDDLE CLASS	POOR
1. Financial Education	Academics	No Education /Academics
2. Create Ideas	Execute Ideas	No Ideas
3. Producer Mentality	Consumer Mentality	Consumer Mentality
4. Money work for them	Work for money	Work for money
5. Applied Learning-Earn	Learn-Earn	Earn-Learn
6. Solution-Centered	Problem-Centered	Problem-Centered
7. Trailers	Complainers	Toilers
8. Live on Investment	Live on salary & pension	Live on working hard
9. Own Business	Manage another's business	No Business
10. Boss (Job Creators)	Boys (Job Seekers)	Victim (Job hunters)

Notes

Notes

www.ingramcontent.com/pod-product-compliance
Lightning Source LLC
Chambersburg PA
CBHW020456160726
47991CB00007B/2680